STAYING BACK

Triad Publishing Company   Gainesville, Florida

STAYING BACK

By Janice Hale Hobby
with Gabrielle Rubin and Daniel Rubin

Illustrated by Carol Richardson

A Message to Parents
by Barry M. Dym, Ph.D.

Library of Congress Cataloging in Publication Data
Hobby, Janice Hale, 1950—
    Staying back.
    Summary: Presents the true stories of seven
elementary school children who shared the difficult
experience of repeating a grade and were helped to
become successful students with a constructive
approach to their problems.
    1. Grade repetition — Juvenile literature.
2. Handicapped children — Education—Juvenile
literature.
1. Grade repetition — 2. Underachievers — I.
Rubin, Gabrielle — II. Rubin, Daniel — III.
Richardson, Carol, ill. — IV. Title
LB3063.H57—1982   372.12'8   82-13526
ISBN 0-937404-00-4
ISBN 0-937404-16-0 (pbk.)

Published and distributed by Triad Publishing Company, Inc.
1110 N.W. 8th Avenue, Gainesville, Florida 32601

For Jason and Mom

The idea for this book came from an original story written by Matthew Reimer after he repeated the 3rd grade. His story, in words and pictures, is printed in its original form.

THESE ARE THE KIDS WHO STAYED BACK

BILLY

When Mom said to wake up, I used to hide under the blanket. "Come on, Billy, get up. I don't have time for this. You're going to be late for school again." Then she'd yank off the blanket and start dressing me.

Sometimes I would get to school on time, and sometimes I wouldn't. If I was late, the other kids would be working when I came in. Miss Fisher would say, "Well, Billy, you'll just have to make up the work you missed." I'd take some paper, but instead of working I usually just drew pictures.

Almost every day my teacher would say, "Where is your phonics worksheet, Billy?" or "Where is your arithmetic? If you don't finish, you'll have to stay in from recess." I didn't really try very hard because I didn't like recess. I was one of the smallest people in my class and I was terrible at games. When I tried to play football with the guys, everyone always jumped on me.

When the class counted all together by fives, nobody could tell that I didn't know how. I didn't care. I didn't want to be there anyway. I liked playing at home with my trucks.

And everyone was six and I was only five and a half.

At the end of the year, my teacher wrote something in cursive on my report card. When I asked my mom about it, all she said was, "Wait until Daddy gets home." So I went outside and played on the jungle gym.

When Daddy came home they told me. "Your teacher wrote a note to us on your report card. She would like you to stay in 1st grade one more year. We think it would be a good idea."

11

First grade again? Why did I have to do 1st grade all over again. I yelled, "FIRST GRADE IS STUPID!" I didn't care about dinner anymore. I felt worse than I ever did in my whole life.

When I started crying, Mom pulled me onto her lap and hugged me. "This is really sad for you, isn't it?" she said. It hurts and makes you feel bad." I nodded. I was still crying a little bit, but I was glad she understood. I told her that I'd miss all the kids in my class. We talked about them. "Don't worry. You'll have lots of new friends," she said. She wrapped her arms around me and held me tight.

Then they started telling me the good parts about repeating.

Daddy said, "You won't be the youngest person in the class anymore."

Mom said, "You need a chance to catch up. School will be more fun for you."

My parents made it sound like repeating 1st grade would be a lot better than going on to 2nd. I decided it would be O.K. I would stay back.

This year I like going to school! Sometimes I get dressed even before my mom tells me.

I read better, and I'm starting to write sentences. Miss Fisher let me read the class a story I wrote. Lots of times I finish my work early. Then I get to do special things, like passing out papers or taking notes to the office.

I used to hate recess, but now it's fun. I'm better at games. I'm not even the shortest person anymore.

I'm seven and some of the other people are seven, and some are six. I like being one of the oldest. My friends don't even tease me about staying back. In fact, I bet everybody's forgotten.

My new report card says, "Promoted to the 2nd grade."

And I'm not staying back again.

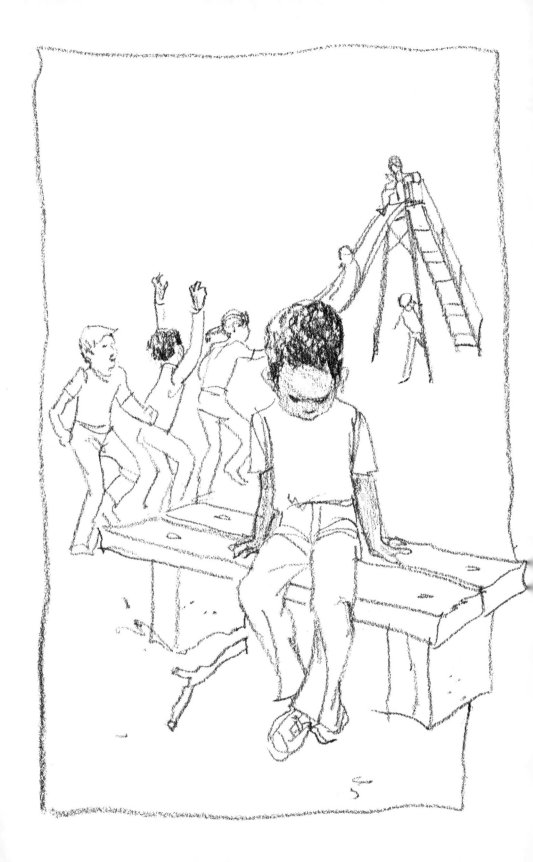

LYNDON

The boys were running and jumping and having a good time. They chased the girls all over the playground — from the fort, to the swings, to the slides. I tried to keep up, but I ran out of breath.

"Come on, Lyndon! No Kings-X!"

"What's wrong with him?"

"Get up, Lyndon. We need you to help us."

The teacher looked over at us. "You kids leave Lyndon alone. You know he's got sickle cell."

"Sickle-cell, pickle-cell. Watch out that the pickle-cell doesn't get you!"

I jumped up and grabbed a stick. "Go on and leave me alone!" I sat down on the bench and tried to catch my breath. There goes another recess, I thought.

I was always missing out on something. Having sickle cell disease means I am almost always too tired to do what everybody else is doing. Sometimes I can't get out of bed in the morning and I miss the whole day, not just on school days but on weekends, too.

When we got back to the room after recess, everyone started asking me questions. Miss Little had told them about sickle cell before, but sometimes they forgot.

"What does it feel like?" asked Toni. Toni always asked dumb questions.

"Sometimes it doesn't feel like anything. But sometimes it hurts bad ... in my legs ... or my feet ... or my stomach ..."

"What *is* a sickle cell, anyway?" Robbie was our class scientist and always wanted to know everything.

"It's a blood cell that's shaped funny."

"How did you know you had it? Did you catch it from somebody?" Robbie asked.

"The doctor told my parents when I was a baby. You don't catch it; you're born with it."

"I hope my babies don't get it," said Susan.

"They can't get it 'cause you're white. Only black babies can have it."

My friend Jerome thinks I'm lucky to be getting out of school so much, but I don't think it's any fun at all. I'm way behind the rest of the class all the time. And I never know what's going on.

My best days are when I do things with the class. Once the teacher asked everyone to think about "when I'm afraid" and draw a picture about it. Judy drew a Halloween picture with ghosts and witches all over the page. John was afraid of a mean dog on his street and drew a big dog with gigantic teeth. I watched Susan rubbing a black crayon all over her paper.

"What's that supposed to be?" I asked her.

"I'm afraid of the dark," she whispered.

When it was my turn I held up a picture of me in the hospital, and a nurse was holding a BIG needle. "I'm afraid of those needles when I go to the hospital," I said.

"I don't like it when I get a shot," said Susan.

"I don't either," said Andrew.

"I don't either," said Charles.

Everyone started talking about hospitals and doctors. When the bell rang, they were still talking.

Robbie walked home with me after school. "Hey, Lyndon! You had the scariest picture. I hope you don't get sick anymore."

Every now and then I have a bad attack, and then my parents take me to the hospital. Usually I come right

home after the doctor sees me, but one time I was stuck there for three weeks. The doctors and nurses were pretty nice, but I sure hated getting all those shots. I'm more scared of needles than anything.

My teacher came to visit me in the hospital once. She brought me some books with the reading assignments and she showed my mama how to work with me on handwriting and other stuff. But I felt so tired I couldn't even sit up to do the work.

The whole year went on like that: in school, out of school, in school, out of school. Even if I had a cold, I'd have to stay home until I was better.

When school ended, Miss Little called Mama and Daddy and me in for a conference. She said that I was behind in everything because I had missed 53 days of school. She wanted them to help her decide if she should pass me on to the next grade.

Mama frowned and said, "What if he misses more school next year?"

"He could have a hard time catching up. Third grade moves faster than 2nd," said Miss Little.

"Then it's settled," said my daddy. "You keep him in 2nd until he's learned everything he's supposed to know." Mama nodded.

I thought that was pretty creepy, making their own son flunk 2nd grade. But I couldn't do anything about it, just like I couldn't help my sickle cell attacks.

This year I'm doing 2nd grade over again. It isn't so bad. Everything is a little easier and I know all my subjects better. Miss Little is my teacher again. She put me in a higher reading group and I'm keeping up!

I'm getting better at working by myself. That way, I don't get behind when I have to stay at home. But the days I can go to school are the very best days of all.

LILLY

It was the first day of school, and the building was filled with children hurrying in every direction. My mother and I were walking to my class with Miss Johnson, the school counselor. Suddenly, everyone started disappearing into the rooms. I looked at my mother. She told me that the bell had rung, meaning that classes were about to start. I got so nervous I could hardly stand up.

"Come on," she said. "It will be okay."

"Can't I go back to the deaf school?" I looked around as the halls got emptier and emptier. I felt my mother pulling me around to look at her.

"Did you get that?" she asked. I shook my head. She repeated, "I just said: your teachers and your father and I think you're ready to go to a school with children who can hear. You have to start sometime. Today is the day."

"I'm scared!" I cried. "I'll be the only deaf person in the class."

"Don't worry, honey. You'll do great. You're a good lip reader and you're good at listening for sounds through your hearing aids. And we'll help you whenever you have problems, just like always." She pulled a Kleenex out of her purse and wiped my eyes. "You're ready, Lilly. Come on."

I nodded, and we walked down the hall to the 3rd grade class. My teacher was Mr. Whitney and my special language teacher was Mrs. Dunn. I had met them before, when my parents first decided to put me in a regular school, so I knew what they looked like. But as soon as we got into Mr. Whitney's room I almost started to cry. *Mr. Whitney had grown the biggest mustache I had ever seen!* It started under his nose and covered both of his lips. How would I ever know what he was saying?

I saw Miss Johnson say something to him. He looked at me, smiled, and nodded. Then he said something to the whole class and left the room. Miss Johnson started to introduce me to everyone.

"Lilly can't *hear* you talk," she said, "but she will understand you as long as she can *see* you when you talk. She wears hearing aids, but they only help a little." The kids seemed friendly and kind of excited to have a deaf person in the class. Just then Mr. Whitney came

back. He had cut his mustache so it didn't cover his mouth. I could see his lips perfectly. He looked straight at me.

"Is that better, Lilly?"

I smiled.

I sat in the front row so I could see Mr. Whitney's face when he spoke. Everyone was very helpful and waited until I turned around before answering a question, so I could read their lips. They also helped by pointing to the person who was going to speak next.

But after a few weeks they seemed to forget that I needed help. Sometimes Mr. Whitney wrote on the blackboard and started asking questions without facing me, and people forgot to wait for me to turn around to see them when they answered. At first I asked them to repeat things, but it got embarrassing to do that all the time, so I usually just sat there.

Lunchtime and recess were the hardest parts of the day. When the kids had food in their mouths I couldn't read their lips. And at recess, everyone was always running around and yelling from far away. At least I had Julie to play with when I didn't want to run with the other kids.

Julie is my best friend. The first time she came to my house, we went upstairs and I put on some records.

"Records?" she exclaimed. "How can you hear records?"

"I can't really *hear* them," I said, "but I can feel the rhythm when the sound is turned way up. They're fun to dance to." Then Julie and I danced around the room to the music.

Some of the kids didn't like talking with me because my speech sounds kind of funny, but most people who know me understand what I say. If Julie is around when there's a problem, she helps. But Julie isn't there all the time, and she can't help me very much during class.

One day my dad said, "Mr. Whitney is worried about your school work. He wants to know if there is anything he can do to help."

"Everything's fine," I said. I didn't want him to know I was having trouble.

Too many times Mr. Whitney seemed to mumble the assignments or say them too quickly. "Do you understand, Lilly?"

"Yes," I would lie. I didn't want him to think I was stupid.

Mrs. Dunn came to school every day to help me with language and vocabulary, but I still wasn't keeping up with the class. By the end of the year I was one of the best students in math and spelling, but I was so far behind in everything else that Mr. Whitney called a meeting with me and my parents.

The conversation went so fast it was hard to follow what was going on. I saw my mother say, "She may be deaf but she's a smart girl." And I saw Mr. Whitney say, "We think she'd be better off in a special class." Then Dad said something like, "Lilly just needs time to adjust," and Mr. Whitney said, "I think you may be right."

"What are you talking about?" I asked.

My mother turned to me. "We all think it would be best for you to repeat the 3rd grade."

Repeat? I couldn't! I'd never failed at anything before in my life. "I won't, I won't, I won't," I screamed. I ran around the room kicking over the desks and throwing the erasers against the wall. My father ran after me and picked me up. He gave me a big hug.

"Don't cry," he said. "You haven't failed."

"Yes I have," I said.

"No you haven't. We knew that your first class with kids who hear would be hard. And we think you've done a great job."

"But what about my friends? What about Julie?"

"You can still see Julie at recess and lunch time," said Mr. Whitney.

"And after school," said my mom. "Besides, you'll make new friends, just like you always have."

"I know I have to be more careful when I talk," said Mr. Whitney. "I can also write down all the assignments for you." I wiped my eyes on my father's sleeve. Mr. Whitney winked at me. "Next September is a new start for both of us. I wouldn't be surprised if you became the best student in the class."

I knew if I tried hard I could be as good as any hearing person in that class at everything, including reading. And I was going to get so good at understanding people that they would hardly even know I wasn't just like everybody else.

When school started again, I went back to the same classroom. Mr. Whitney was still my teacher, but he looked a little different. The mustache!

"Hi, Lilly," he smiled.

"You shaved it off!"

His eyes twinkled and he started to laugh. "You said you could understand me with my mustache, but I know you never liked it. We're going to have a good year together."

I skipped back to my seat. Those were the nicest words I had ever "heard."

JENNIFER

I never told my parents anything about school. They really didn't want to know, anyway. If they asked: "Don't you have any homework tonight?," I'd say: "I did it at school." That was enough to get them off my back for a while. Anyone could have figured out I was lying, but they didn't bother to listen.

Sometimes when the house was quiet I would look out of the window and dream about living in the country and riding horses, or wearing pretty dresses to lots of parties. Then I'd hear the front door slam. Dad was home, and all the yelling would start up again.

First, Mom would scream at him. "Where are the groceries I asked you to pick up? What are we supposed to eat ... air?"

Then he would holler back at her. "Get them yourself! I work all day long. Do I have to come home to a dirty house and a nagging wife?"

And Mom would yell, "You're not the only one who works. Or doesn't that count?"

Then Dad would yell, "All you ladies do in that office is gossip all day long. What's so hard about that?"

Then Mom would start crying and say, "You are the meanest, most selfish man I ever met!"

The arguments always ended with Dad yelling, "If you don't like it, you don't have to stay. *Why don't you just take your stupid kid and get out of here!*"

He always said that when he got mad. He always
said I was stupid. I buried my face in the pillow.

Home was terrible, but school was worse. I couldn't
ever concentrate on what the teacher was saying.
Sometimes I fell asleep in class. Mrs. Allen wrote notes
to my parents, but I tore them up as soon as I got
outside the door. I didn't want to give them anything
new to fight about.

When my report card came with all D's I was scared out of my wits. My parents *couldn't* see that ... no way! I carefully traced my mom's name at the bottom of the card and returned it to the teacher the next morning.

Only she caught me. It was horrible. She gave me a lecture about being dishonest and said she had to tell my mother.

"Come with me, Jennifer," she ordered as soon as the three o'clock bell rang. I wanted to run, but Mrs. Allen took my hand and led me to the office. She picked up the phone and quickly dialed 5-5-5-4-8-9-1. I held my breath and wished as hard as I could that Mom wouldn't be there.

"Hello, Mrs. Greenley. This is Mrs. Allen, Jennifer's teacher. How are you?" My heart was thumping so loud I could barely hear what she was saying.

"I'm sorry to bother you, but I think you should know about some serious problems Jennifer is having." She told my mom about everything — the notes, the report card, the bad grades, *everything*. Then she said, "I really have no choice. I will have to put Jennifer's name on the list for repeating 4th grade."

After that, Mrs. Allen just listened to the phone. She was shaking her head. Finally she said, "I'm sorry to hear that. Jennifer's got so many problems on top of the divorce . . . ."

DIVORCE! WHAT DIVORCE? What was she talking about? Were my parents getting a divorce? Would Mom tell my teacher and not tell me? Was it because they knew about the report card? I felt tears roll down my cheeks.

I looked up at Mrs. Allen, hoping that she would stop talking and let me go home. When she saw me crying, she looked at me kind of funny; then she put her arms around me. "I'm so sorry, Jennifer. I thought you knew."

It was like a horrible dream. I ran all the way home and fell on my bed. I lay there for hours, listening for the door slam that meant Dad was home, but it never came.

That was the worst year of my life. My parents got divorced, my dad moved out, and I flunked. I kept hoping that Dad would come back home, but he never did. I thought for a long time that it was all my fault since they fought about me so much, but Mom said it wasn't and I shouldn't think that.

Mom was nicer after Dad left. She started talking to me more often. Not yelling, just talking. She kept saying that things were going to get better. I missed Dad, but I didn't miss the yelling. I hoped this was the end of my bad year.

September came, school started, and I was still in the 4th grade. I was glad I didn't have Mrs. Allen again, although it was kind of scary starting all over with someone new. The whole class was so different! Lots of the stuff we studied was the same, but this time Ms. Watson helped me do all the hard work I had goofed up on last year.

One day Ms. Watson came over to check my math problems. "Jennifer, that's fantastic! You got every one right!" she said, and everyone in the class heard her. I felt embarrassed at first, but actually I kind of liked hearing it.

"You know, Jennifer, you're a pretty smart young lady." Was she talking to me? It was the first time anyone had ever said I was smart. I decided to work hard and start showing everyone how easy this 4th grade stuff was, and by the end of the first six weeks I won the "Good Speller" award. I wasn't afraid to take that home!

Mom smiled and hugged me. "Let's go shopping, Jennifer. Let's buy you a new dress." When we got home from the store, I phoned Dad. He said he was really proud of me. After dinner, Mom did the dishes so I could do my homework.

Things kept getting better, and by the first report card I had two A's and three B's. I had to look at the name twice to make sure I didn't have the wrong card.

"Look at this! Look at this!" I waved the card at Sandy, who sat next to me.

"You're kidding!"

"No, it's mine!" I was so excited I couldn't wait to take my report card home. But before I could leave school there was someone else I had to show, someone who needed to see that Jennifer was not so dumb.

I felt my stomach knot up as I walked down the hall. When I got to Mrs. Allen's room, I ran up to her desk waving my report card in front of me like a big flag. The A's and B's jumped right out at her.

"Wow! What a report card!" Mrs. Allen said, the same way she did when she talked to her favorite students.

"I knew you could do it! Now tell me, who do you think is the most improved student in 4th grade this year?"

"Me, Mrs. Allen! I am!" I shouted. I didn't care if the whole school heard. I didn't care if the whole world heard!

CHIP

"*The chil - dren but ...*"

"*Put.*"

"*The chil - dren put on the - their dath - bath - ing ...*"

"*BATHE - ing suits!*" *snapped Mrs. Norton.* "*You KNEW this yesterday. What's wrong with you?*"

"*The chil - dren but - put ...*"

"*Okay, Chip, that's IT. I can't sit here all day while you sound out every single word. I've got 30 other students. Just let me know when you're ready to stop playing games.*"

I threw the book down on my desk as hard as I could. Mrs. Norton just didn't understand me. Every day she went over the reading with me and every day I messed up. She said she didn't know how I could forget the words so fast, and neither did I. Everyone else could read, *really read,* even hard words like "transportation" and "encyclopedia."

For a long time I tried hard to read too, but the letters always seemed to play tricks on me. My eyes got so tired, I didn't know where a word started or stopped. But the teacher didn't believe that I was really trying. Every time I couldn't do what she wanted she'd get mad. I got mad, too. Finally, I just quit.

After that, she left me alone. She said she hoped I would get tired of sitting and start working. Well, I wasn't going to work for HER. I just sat there and stared out the window.

The whole rest of the year I knew that I was going to fail. It became a joke. Someone would say, "That assignment's too hard — let's give it to Chip." "Yeah, give it to the genius." And then everyone would look at me and laugh. I acted like I didn't care, but it really made me mad.

My next report card was more horrible than usual. My parents tried to understand, but it didn't make any sense to them. I think they felt as bad as I did. Mom tried to cheer me up.

"You're not the only person who's ever had a hard time in school, Chip. Don't worry. You'll catch on soon."

My sister Jane said, "Maybe I can get my teacher to help you like she helps me when I have trouble with something."

But no matter what they said, I felt like the dumbest kid that ever lived.

My parents talked for days about my school work and Mrs. Norton and everything. Finally, they told me, "We've called the counselor's office. The counselor has made an appointment for you to see Dr. West, the school psychologist."

Dr. West was really nice. She asked me a lot of questions about school. She had me read and write a little.

When we were finished she said, "Chip, you've probably been pretty frustrated and discouraged that you still have to struggle so much to read."

Finally! Someone understood!

She told Dad: "Chip has a learning disability that makes it hard for him to read.

She was great. She KNEW that "saw" looked the same to me as "was" and that b's and d's and p's all looked alike. It was just like she'd climbed inside my head.

Dr. West said that I was just as smart as other people my age and told us about the Pineview School, an ungraded private school where they help kids like me. I wasn't so sure I believed the part about being smart, but I wanted to.

So, instead of failing 5th, I started going to Pineview. At first I thought it was fun having so much special attention. But the teachers always picked my worst problems to work on, and that was hard to take all the time.

After awhile I finally started liking Pineview. We tape recorded my voice while I was reading and kept graphs of what I learned. We also played a lot of games. The teachers gave me interesting books with stories about sports and great athletes, and I got to write letters to the astronauts and other famous people. I started to like science. Now I even have a favorite subject — geology.

Nobody laughs at me anymore. At Pineview they don't point you out and put you down. With a class full of kids who are all having problems, it's the one who thinks he knows everything who gets put down. I learned it was okay to make mistakes as long as I tried.

I don't know what will happen when I leave Pineview. What grade will they put me in? Will I always have to work twice as hard as everyone else?

My teacher told me that Winston Churchill had a learning disability, and so did Albert Einstein.

Well, I guess if they could make it, so can I!

RYAN

I never wanted to move to Florida. Things were just fine back in Deerfield. All my friends said they'd write to me, but you just can't play ball or mess around in a letter. After only a week I already missed my old school and my old neighborhood. And 5th grade had been so much fun; it wasn't fair getting pulled out right in the middle of the year.

The new school must have been ten times as big as my old school. As my mom and I walked down the hall I could hear our footsteps echoing, and every classroom we passed had its doors closed so I couldn't see what was going on inside. My brother Eric had been all excited when we dropped him off at his new 3rd grade class. Boy, what a jerk!

When we came to Mrs. Hackett's class, my mom gave me a quick kiss, squeezed my shoulders, and started walking back down the hall. "Have fun!" she called. "See you after school."

I took a hard swallow and opened the door. Mrs. Hackett looked kind of annoyed when she saw me. I was interrupting, I guess.

"You must be Ryan. Come on in. We're expecting you." At least she knew who I was, even though I still felt that I wasn't in the right place. "Please take the seat over there," she pointed. I hadn't even finished sitting down when she started teaching again.

Everything here was so strict. Don't chew gum, don't talk, raise your hand, stay in your seat — rules, rules, rules! My teacher back in Deerfield was so friendly. This place wasn't any fun at all.

Lunch time should have been a good break from sitting in class, but in some ways it was even worse. On one side of the room near the food line was the "in" table, and on the other side near the garbage were the "creeps." The "in" table was for the kids who were really cool, like Danny Clark. I wasn't invited to sit with them, and I didn't want to be a creep, so I usually sat alone.

P.E. wasn't any better. Back in Deerfield I was pretty good in sports, especially in 16-inch softball, but they didn't even play that here. Danny Clark and Jeff Something-or-other always got to be team captains just because they were popular. I always got picked last. I was going to show them all that I was as good as any of them, but it seemed the harder I tried, the worse I got.

"Don't throw the ball to Ryan; he'll just drop it," someone would say.

"Oh, no, are we stuck with Ryan?"

"Ryan, Ryan, always cryin'!" sang one of the creeps. "Ryan, Ryan, always cryin'!" When I heard that guy I turned around and decked him. I got sent to the principal's office, but at least hardly anyone bothers me any more.

The worst part about the new school was that everybody was ahead of me, especially in math. Back in Deerfield we weren't going to do percents until the end of 5th grade, but here they had already had it. Sometimes I didn't even bother looking at the homework since I knew I wouldn't understand it. Why couldn't we just go back to Deerfield?

My parents were really upset when they found out how bad I was doing. "Ryan, you're just not pushing yourself hard enough," said my mom. "If you'd try harder, you would do better."

Dad nodded. "Mrs. Hackett says you got into another fight today. What was that all about?"

"The guy was a creep," I said.

"You didn't hit the creeps in Deerfield."

"So let's go back there," I pleaded. "I liked Deerfield."

My Dad took a quarter out of his pocket and gave it to me. "So long, son. Have a nice trip."

"Quit joking; I'm serious."

"Ryan, your mom, your brother, and I live *here* now. We'd kind of like you to stay with us."

"But I hate it here."

"You're just going to have to keep trying. Eric likes the new school. He's getting along just fine."

"Oh, sure! He's only in 3rd grade. That's easy stuff. I bet he wouldn't like 5th grade too much."

My Dad stopped smiling and leaned forward in his chair. "Look, Ryan. If you don't get those grades up you're going to flunk. It's as easy as that."

The next day I tried working harder, but it didn't seem to help. I did make a few friends, and Danny Clark even turned out to be pretty nice, except when the other kids were around. But I still got into too many fights, and when I got mad I couldn't concentrate on my work. By the end of the year I felt like I hadn't learned anything. I couldn't wait for school to be over.

One day Mrs. Hackett called me up to her desk. "It's been a tough year for you, hasn't it?" she said. I was going to say, "Yeah, thanks to you," but I was too scared.

"I want to talk to you about Danny Clark for a minute," she said. Danny Clark? I thought. Why would she want to tell me anything about him? "Did you know this is Danny's second time in 5th grade? Did you know he's repeating?"

The most popular kid in the class? No kidding! I couldn't believe it!

"There's something else, Ryan," she said. Here it comes, I thought. "I'd like you to do 5th grade over again too." I felt my face turning a little red, so I turned away from her and looked out the window. "Now that you know your way around the school, and you know the way we do things here, you won't have to worry about getting adjusted again. And now that you'll be starting fresh along with the rest of the class, nobody will be ahead of anybody else. I think you'll do just fine."

I nodded to her and walked out of the room. At first I felt pretty awful, but in a way I was relieved. I only hoped my dad wouldn't be mad.

"We already know," he said when I told him that evening. "Your teacher called us this afternoon." He lifted the newspaper from his lap and folded it. Gee. He wasn't taking it so bad at all.

"Lots of people get held back in school," said my mom. "Right, dear?" She was nudging my father with her elbow. "Right?"

Finally, my dad put down his paper and started laughing. "You know something, Ryan," he said. "When I was your age I had to repeat a grade myself." We all started laughing. Wow! My own father!

So, I repeated 5th grade. Sometimes I felt like a dummy for flunking, but nobody else even seemed to care. I guess people forget pretty fast and just start treating you like everybody else. And that's all I really wanted in the first place.

RONNIE

My full name is Ronald James Hobson the Third. My father, Ronald James Hobson the Second, doesn't think I'm doing well enough in school. He says my grandfather, Ronald James Hobson the First, would have been plenty unhappy to know about the grades I've been getting.

"My grades are mostly average. What's wrong with that?" I would ask.

"You're a Hobson," he would say. "And you should be doing better in school. Now, upstairs with you. You have some studying to do."

Why couldn't my parents leave me alone? Every time I turned around there was a new tutor to help me in math or reading. They kept after my teacher, Mrs. Harvey, to spend more time with me, but that only made her treat me like I was some kind of spoiled brat. The same thing had happened every single year, and by 6th grade it was driving me nuts.

What really bugged me was that my parents had my whole life planned out for me, all the way through college. Well, I had news for them. I wasn't *going* to college.

"You just don't care at all what *I* want to do," I'd say. "You just don't care."

"That's not true," my dad would say. "You can do anything you want. As long as you're the BEST."

Sometimes I wish I had another family. Most of my friends get about the same grades I do but their parents never bother them about it.

When I can, I like to go to John's house. His father does interesting things with him instead of making him work every minute of the day. They have this terrific workshop and all kinds of tools and equipment. When I go over there John's father helps us build things. We built a dog house that looks just like John's house, only smaller.

My parents don't even know what it's like to have fun. They think that just because *they* work hard, I have to suffer too.

So it's always "upstairs with you," whenever I get home from school. My mother keeps coming into my room to look over my shoulder while I work. But I keep doing my own things when she's not looking.

Why couldn't my parents just let me be myself? Fat chance! Even my name isn't my own — Ronald James Hobson THE THIRD!

All through 6th grade my parents got more and more uptight and kept pushing me to do better. The more they tried, the worse my grades got, and by the end of the year I flunked right out of 6th grade. At least I did that myself.

That summer, my parents put me in a fancy private school so I could catch up. Well, that didn't work either. By the end of the summer they finally gave up.

"We've done everything we can for you, Ronald," cried my mother. "We have no choice but to allow you to repeat the 6th grade."

"I hope we can keep it from getting around town," muttered my father. "Imagine, a Hobson flunking school."

After that, they left me alone. I don't know if they just gave up, or if someone at the school told them they weren't helping any by pushing so much. All I know is that when school started again there were no more tutors and no more standing over my shoulder and "upstairs with you." No more bugging my teacher and no more bugging me.

This year, instead of sitting and staring at my homework after school, I play soccer or baseball. On weekends, I usually go over to John's house. I found out I really liked building things, and I've become pretty good at it. I made my mom a jewelry box for her birthday. I think it was the first time I ever did anything that impressed my parents.

The same kind of thing happened at school. With nobody telling me what I should be good at, I found out for myself what I liked. My new teacher, Mr. Jordan, helped a lot. He has friends all over the world who write to him, and he brings the envelopes with the foreign stamps to school. Our classroom is filled with picture books about the places his letters come from.

When Mr. Jordan saw that I was a little bit interested in the United Nations stamps, he brought in a lot of different kinds and GAVE them to me! That sure helped me with geography. Mr. Jordan doesn't seem to mind spending time with me, I guess because no one is telling him that he has to.

When my parents saw that I was doing some things pretty well, they realized I wasn't such an embarrassment to the family. I still may be Ronald James Hobson the Third. But now there's a difference. I'm *me* ... just plain "Ronnie."

Matthew's Story

One day I noticed that I was one
of the smallest people in our class

1

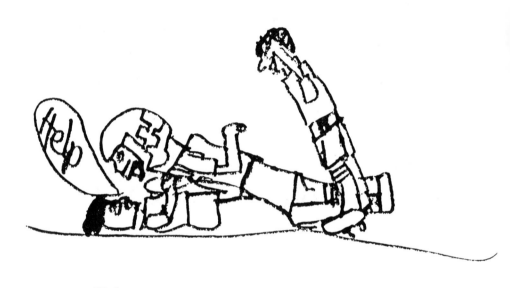

I got jumped on in football.

2

I only made 4 home runs and
I only scored 10 runs I was
out 100 times I think in kickball

I only made it too the sixes in multiplication.

4

Time to change

And I never finished my seatwork 5
on time

Brithday list

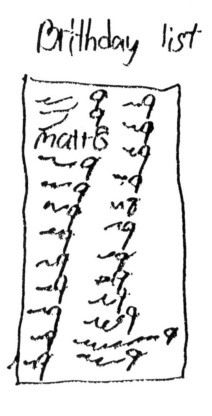

And every one was 9 and I was only 8.

6

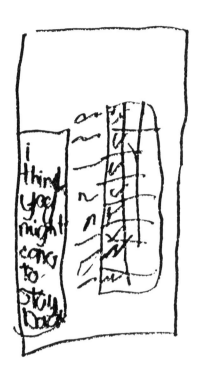

And one of my report card it sugges ged
that I stay back. And I was very sad t

7

I talked about it with my mom and Dad
and I decided to stayback.

And now Im not the shortest
person in our class

And I don't get jumped on in
football,

And I made 20 home runs
and I was out only 20 times
   and I scored 50 times

And I passed my 12's in
multiplication

And now I fnish my seatwork
on time

And now Im good a lot
   of other people are 9 to
   and some are 8 too   8

And Im not staying back again

And I'm very happy I did. And I i met t some new friends tcd.

Paley
me
q

Promoted,
to 4ᵀʰ grade.

Matthew Reimer repeated 3rd grade. By staying back he had a chance to grow up a little and be ready for the work and play of his class. He also took the opportunity to write the story that became this book.

Today, Matthew feels good about what happened. Looking back on how that extra year in school affected him, this is what he says about it:

As I look back at my experience of repeating third grade, I believe that it was one of the most significant events in my life. My whole life changed.

I was transformed from a follower to a leader, from a watcher to a doer. It was easier to make friends and to be a part of the group. I was able to participate in sports, and I became very good in baseball.

I was the kicker for my high school's football team and was a co-captain of the baseball team. My grades improved as I was able to complete my work faster and more easily.

In June of 1989, I graduated with a B+ average from high school, where I served on the Student Council, was the photographer and assistant sports editor for the school newspaper, and played in the jazz band. I won a writing award in the 11th grade and a journalism award for "Story of the Year" in the 12th grade.

I have just completed my freshman year in college; I played baseball while earning all A's and B's in my courses.

I believe that repeating third grade gave me the time to mature and develop at my own pace, making all of my other accomplishments possible. I have never regretted that extra year.

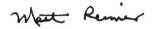

A MESSAGE TO PARENTS

By Barry M. Dym, Ph.D.

The decision to hold a child back in school almost always produces a crisis in the family. Rarely coming "out of the blue," it is often the culmination of a long and painful process that has left everyone feeling confused and helpless. Naturally, the child is upset, filled with feelings of failure, disappointment, and frustration. As a parent you can be similarly affected, thrown off balance with a sense of failure and nervousness about the future. It is difficult to imagine turning this complex crisis into a positive experience for child and family.

You can, however, take steps to help your child transform school failure into an opportunity for growth and self-affirmation. Here are my suggestions.

STEP ONE: Let your child know you love her.

Make clear statements — words, hugs, actions — whatever is right for you.

STEP TWO: Listen. Before offering reassurances or suggestions, let your child talk freely and express as much or as little of his feelings as he can or wishes to share.

Your child needs to air these thoughts and feelings — fears, hopes, ideas of what is real. For an emotionally charged event such as being kept back, talking freely is even more important. When children "hold in" their thoughts, they are left with distorted ideas of themselves as being bad or stupid. These thoughts can fester and show up as depression or even burst out as behavior problems. Just being able to talk openly in your presence will help your child feel safer and better accepted.

This is not easy, because you may feel anxious yourself. You may identify with your child's "failure" and feel sad or angry yourself. You may see the pain on your child's face and wish to lash out at someone — a teacher, a husband or wife, another child, or perhaps the child who has been left back. After all, he is the source of his parents' anguish. At a time like this it is hard to just listen to children. We all want to *do* something.

Just listening is an art. There will be time later to act. If your child says he feels stupid, you may wish to jump in and deny it. Don't. Perhaps give him a hug. For the moment, let him express his fears and doubts. Even though staying back does not necessarily mean he is stupid or lazy, it does signal a failure, and he knows this. Before you can help him move beyond his sense of failure, you need to let him feel it. He needs to acknowledge his true feelings about himself without worrying about how painful this may be to you. When he gains the unflinching knowledge of your acceptance, he may then be ready and willing to do something about his "failure."

STEP THREE: *Try to identify exactly what staying back means to your child. How does he see himself? This will give you the information you need to help turn the disappointment around into something positive.*

Each of the children in the book had their worst fears confirmed . . . of being stupid, unlikeable, inadequate, or sickly. A child can get stuck in a vicious cycle: a poor self-image leads to anxiety in the classroom, which leads to poor performance, which reinforces the poor self-image. If you can identify how your child now sees himself, you can work on that image as a way to break this cycle.

STEP FOUR: *Explore what your child's staying back means to you and to other family members.*

Your child will wonder about this. But before you can help, you may have to step back and think about what failure means to you personally. Do you feel defeated and depressed? Do you blame others — perhaps others who are conveniently close by, like a family member? Perhaps a big institution like the schools or the government? Most people do a little of each of these before coming up with a realistic picture of the situation and deciding what to do next.

Whatever your style of dealing with failure, you should realize that your feelings are normal, and that even wild thoughts, like giving up and running away, are also normal. You should try to understand and separate *your* thoughts and feelings about this failure from those of your child, so they won't get in the way when you try to communicate with the child about being left back.

Failure is often embarrassing to parents and they keep their own failures hidden as much as possible. But if you can share some of your own experiences of failure with your child, she will have a model of how grown people whom she thinks of as strong and competent could also have failed. If there are two parents, each might try this, so that she has more than one model. If she can identify with your failure, hers won't become a painful wedge between you.

STEP FIVE: *Using your child's own ideas, "reframe" the experience of being kept back as an opportunity to succeed. For example, it may be the chance to stop struggling on the bottom rung of a class.*

Having listened to your child, reflected on your own feelings, and shared some of your own experiences, it is now time to try to turn around the meaning of staying back, to help transform failure into opportunity. You will find examples in the stories of how staying back can be treated as a "break." For Billy it was a chance to stop being the smallest and slowest boy in his class. For Ryan, it was an opportunity to recover the self-confidence he lost in the new environment. And for Lilly, whose teacher finally acknowledged her deafness as a problem with which he should be concerned, staying back offered the possibility of being an outstanding student.

These are some general themes you can emphasize in reframing failure as opportunity:

BEFORE, you felt out of control; NOW you take charge of the situation.

BEFORE, you worked under so much pressure that your good qualities couldn't come out.

BEFORE, other people didn't understand you — your special problems and your special virtues — but NOW we can make sure they do.

BEFORE, I (your parent) did not know how much you needed me; failing was your way of telling me this and NOW I know.

BEFORE, you were trying to be like someone else, and that didn't work; NOW you can relax a bit, and with our help you only have to be yourself.

These are only suggestions. There are endless ways to reframe the meaning of what has happened, and you will be able to come up with themes of your own that are tailored to the thoughts and feelings your child expressed during the listening period. Try to use his words and ideas. This is a crucial part of the process and highlights how important the listening phase is. If you just tell him that things will be OK, often he may not believe you. Generalized reassurance can backfire, because he will sense that his feelings are being taken lightly, that you don't understand him, that you are giving him a pat on the head so that you can dismiss him quickly.

STEP SIX: While letting your child "off the hook" of failure, you still need to state firm, clear expectations about hard work for greater success in the future.

There will be times you want to give in to your feelings of helplessness and give up, since, after all, you probably tried hard to avoid this situation. It may help to do this privately or with other adults, and it is even all right to tell your child that you, too, sometimes feel like giving up or angrily lashing out at someone.

In the end, however, you are the parent and in control of the family. Your main job with this child is to let her know that you think she is capable of passing next year and that you expect her to pass. Strangely enough, this expectation firmly stated is more reassuring than just saying that "everything will work out fine."

You can also do more to take charge of the situation. This will probably require spending additional time with teachers, counselors, and principals, until you have worked out a suitable study plan for her for the following year. You must consider whether it is best to continue with the same teacher or in the same school. Think about your child's learning style and find out whether the school district offers classrooms more suited to her needs and abilities.

It may be helpful for you to think about the kind of support you have given her in school so far, and whether your approach to helping her with schoolwork should be different. I am not saying that you have done anything wrong, but I have known many parents, for example, who have helped two or three of their children academically, but found their approach disastrous with the fourth. So experiment a little. If you tend to be tough, try being more lenient. If you are used to giving a lot of responsibility, give her less: monitor her much more carefully. As you experiment, which is really all parents can do, watch to see if the results are good; if she is doing better in school, give yourself a pat on the back and keep it up. If she isn't, try another approach.

STEP SEVEN: Finally, find some ways to pay special attention to the things your child does well.

This will have two benefits: First, it will provide an opportunity to spend "good" time with him; you have probably spent lots of frustrating and upsetting time in the months leading up to his being kept back. Second, this will show him better than words that problems don't reflect all of his personality. Third, success breeds success. The more time he spends with you and with others important to him while he is experiencing himself as competent, the better it is. This confidence-building is likely to spill over into school and other areas of his life.

I know that following these steps will require much thought, hard work, and the courage to experiment. But I believe that most parents are willing to work and experiment if there is a chance of helping their children, even though, in the process, there may be considerable pain and confusion. I hope that these guidelines I have offered you will be helpful as markers on a difficult journey.

LET'S TALK ABOUT STAYING BACK

An open discussion between child and caring adult can help the child with a poor self-image develop a more positive view about himself or herself. Adults can use the following questions about the stories to help children talk about their feelings. The answers are not as important as the feelings and concepts that can evolve as a result of the discussion.

BILLY

Why do you think Billy didn't like school the first time he was in the 1st grade?

What kinds of things did Billy do that showed he didn't like school?

How do you feel about school right now?

The second time Billy was in 1st grade, what was different?

What would help make school better for you?

Billy's story is a good example of how many things can become easier for a child who is held back due to immaturity. The extra year in 3rd grade gave Billy a chance to mature and become more "in-sync" with his classmates, offering him a better chance for success in the classroom and on the playground.

This story also helps adults understand how children feel better about themselves when they experience success in something. Ask your child what he feels successful in. If he has trouble answering, help him find successful activities or skills. Any positive activity will do; it could be as simple as singing, drawing, being a fast runner, or taking care of the family pet. The more difficulty the child has in finding a success, the more important it is to help discover one, no matter how small. Continually build on this by creating or discovering more successful activities later.

LYNDON

If you were Lyndon's mother or father, would you want him to repeat the 2nd grade? How would you tell him?

A child may resent the decision (about repeating) that has been made for him by his teacher or parents. Role-playing can help the child analyze whether or not he, as a parent, would want a student to continue at a pace that would be increasingly difficult.

Do you know why Lyndon started doing better in school, in spite of his illness? What new ability did he feel he developed in order to help himself?

Discuss qualities and abilities a child may have that will give him the best chance of succeeding. In Lyndon's case, he liked school, and he was able to improve his schoolwork by learning to work alone when he was ill. Help your child list ways in which he can help himself during the new school year. Add to that the ways in which you as parent (or teacher or counselor) will be helping. Putting together such a list can help the child feel he is surrounded by people who care and that he has a fighting chance the second time around.

LILLY

What did Lilly's father mean when he told her that she did not fail 3rd grade. In what ways was Lilly successful in 3rd grade?

When children do the best they can, they are *not* failures. Lilly had done well in some of her school subjects, she had made a new friend, and she had adjusted to a new school and new situation.

What do you know about Lilly that you think will help her do better in 3rd grade the second time? In what other ways do you think she will help herself?

The main idea here is that Lilly's determination to be "as good as" children who hear is an important quality for a handicapped child to have or develop. This can help her gain the confidence she needs to be able to ask for help with her schoolwork. *Any* child, even a very young child or one who is not handicapped, can take an active role to improve a difficult situation.

JENNIFER

What happened to make school especially hard for Jennifer when she was in 4th grade the first time? How do you think she felt about herself then?

Falling behind in school is a common problem among children experiencing an emotional problem, such as their parents' divorce. A child coping with or fearing any major disrupting event or pattern at home will probably identify with Jennifer's story. Your child's answers to these questions can be a clue. A discussion of how Jennifer feels can lead to verbalizing underlying fears and worries that your child may be experiencing and will give you a chance to offer assurances or explanations.

What special thing did Jennifer's new teacher tell her that made her decide to try hard to improve her schoolwork? Why was it so important? What other things happened that helped Jennifer feel happier about herself and school?

What kinds of things could help you feel happier about yourself and school?

Children need encouragement and praise to be motivated. Ask your child to describe herself; then work on developing a positive self-image by making a list together of her best traits, making sure to find ways of adding to the list.

CHIP

What did Chip do when the other students made fun of him? How do you think he really felt? How do you think you would have felt and acted?

Chip hid his real feelings and pretended he didn't care when the other children made fun of him. Encourage your child to discuss any real incidents of peer pressure that may have taken place; this will give you a chance to identify possible ways for him to deal with them.

How was Pineview different from Chip's other school? How did that help him? Is reading or schoolwork more difficult for you than for your friends?

Pineview's ungraded system with individualized instruction meant Chip's progress was not compared with that of other students. In addition, he no longer felt different since all the children were having some type of difficulty with schoolwork. Chip's story illustrates how the elimination of continuous frustration can be a factor in helping children with learning disabilities perform better.

Before reading Chip's story, did you know that some famous people had trouble with learning and reading?

A child who finds school very difficult may think that nothing will ever improve. Just knowing that there have been successful people who also had difficulties can help children see that a slow start or a learning problem does not preclude striving toward and achieving goals.

RYAN

What kinds of things made Ryan hate his new school? What did he do that showed he was unhappy?

Have you ever felt like Ryan when you were in a new situation? Do you remember what it was like for you?

A child who has recently transferred to a new school may be feeling very insecure about different or more advanced schoolwork, as well as making new friends and being accepted. Ask your child to list the things that seem strange and difficult in the new school. What could you or he do to help improve any of them? Discuss the positive aspects of the new school. Verbalizing the issues into a concrete list may help him feel more in control of the situation and dispel the ominous feeling that newness can create.

What was it that Ryan's teacher and father each told him that helped him feel better about staying back? How did it help?

It was helpful for Ryan to know that other people, whom he did not view as failures, had also been held back. Try to find incidents from your childhood that made you feel as if you had failed, but which grew to be less significant as you grew older. Let your child know you are not perfect!

RONNIE

What are some of the things that Ronnie's parents did or said to him that bothered him?

What did Ronnie like about working in his friend's workshop?

What activities make you feel good about yourself? How?

Ronnie's story shows how children who do not live up to their parents' expectations of them academically can still achieve in other areas. It also points out the importance of being recognized and valued for one's own individuality. Ask your child what he would like to do well. A discussion of interests may lead both of you to a better understanding of his interests and abilities.

ABOUT THE AUTHORS

Janice Hale Hobby is a teacher of exceptional students at P. K. Yonge Laboratory School at the University of Florida and is working on her doctorate in special education administration. Her more than ten years as an educator have focused upon personalizing instruction for unique learners of all ages in both public and private sectors.

Gabrielle Rubin is a teacher at Gallaudet School for the Deaf in St. Louis and a communications therapist at St. Louis State Hospital.

Daniel Rubin is a freelance writer and part-time instructor at Northwestern University.

Dr. Barry M. Dym, a practicing family therapist, is founder and director of the Family Institute of Cambridge.

Carol Richardson is a watercolorist living in Daytona Beach, Florida.

372.12   Hobby, Janice Hale
Hob
          Staying back

91-901

372.12   Hobby, Janice Hale
Hob
          Staying back

91-901